I0150934

Balzac's Robe and Other Poems

New Women's Voices Series, No. 122

poems by

Laura Marello

Finishing Line Press
Georgetown, Kentucky

Balzac's Robe and Other Poems

New Women's Voices Series, No. 122

ACKNOWLEDGMENTS

This book would not be possible without the assistance of the following
people and institutions: the Stegner Fellowship at Stanford University, the
Fine Arts Work Center Provincetown, MacDowell Colony, the Corporation
of Yaddo, Millay Colony, Montalvo Center for the Arts, Djerassi Foundation,
the Vogelstein Foundation, Deming Foundation, and the Outer Cape
Residency Consortium, with special thanks to Paul Nelson, Donna Graboff,
Janis Barrow, Betty Matthews and Nonnette Sherry.

Editor: Christen Kincaid

Cover Art: Brooke Marcy

Author Photo: Kim Brufford

Cover Design: Elizabeth Maines

Printed in the USA on acid-free paper.
Order online: www.finishinglinepress.com
also available on amazon.com

Author inquiries and mail orders:
Finishing Line Press
P. O. Box 1626
Georgetown, Kentucky 40324
U. S. A.

Table of Contents

for Donna Graboff

Balzac's Robe

He wrote in it.
He was naked underneath.
All day, an enormous man with gargantuan
appetites, his belly protruding. He wrote volumes and
volumes, longhand, naked, in his robe. Later Rodin

made a statue of him that way, naked under his robe. It stands
in the Place Pigalle. He looks like a giant
black penguin. Professional jealousy between rival artists of the
turn of the century, I presume.

Not that it's up to me to
presume, of course. I presume nothing. My credo, as it
were, is to not make assumptions. Assume nothing. Neither
presume nor assume. It's on my door. I'm hanging it up
there now. Right now. I tell you.

Who am I? Oh, that doesn't
matter. What matters is
who you are.
Who Balzac was.
Is—I mean.

True Beige

I had a friend once who hated the
color beige. He was very insistent, not only about
his hatred for beige, but also about the specificity of
the color. My stone pants, he insisted, were not
beige. My taupe sweater was not beige. Likewise, my light brown
waffled comforter cover was not
beige, nor was my honey maple furniture, my cream sheets, my
ivory area rugs—none of these was
beige. Only my file cabinet was
beige, and he despised it.

I have heard of many famous people who
were preoccupied with a particular
color, but usually they were drawn to
the color, not repelled by it. The composer Erik
Satie restricted himself to a white food
diet. He ate white rice, mashed potatoes, milk, white fish, white
bread. The French writer Colette wrote on blue
paper. The American painter Georgia O'Keefe would only
wear black.

True north,
true west, true colors, true blue, true
beige.

Bone White

There was a truck parked outside
my apartment building yesterday, with large gray
plastic tubs of paint in the flatbed. The labels on the
tubs said *bone white*.

I didn't know that bone could
be a description of
white, a kind of white. I guess it
could. I guess if a bone were picked
clean and bleached, it would be a kind
of white. And I suppose the
walls in my newly painted apartment
could be described as bone

white. Though, if you really want to know the
truth, I'd rather not have known. Since I have to live
here, I'd rather just think of them as white, or off—white, or
even ivory.

How to Find Water in the Desert

We tend to forget that Los Angeles is a
desert. I carry water with me everywhere. I carry it in
little plastic bottles with twist-on
caps. Oftentimes I suddenly feel as if I can't speak or
breathe or live another moment if I don't drink some
water.

Growing up we drank tap water with chromium
six in it. We'd hike up into the canyons on Getty Oil land above
our housing tract, and sit under an oak tree until the sun
set. We did not bring water with us. I remember bringing
lunch in a paper sack.

One way to find water in the desert is to locate a stand of
palm trees. Dig. There is a spring of water underneath. A less
    obvious
way to find water in the desert is to locate the nearest
water source, and build a channel from it to
the desert. If the water is five hundred miles away, up
in the mountains, you build a channel five hundred miles, down
into the desert. You can do this, if you
dare, much to the consternation of the people up
in the mountains, who own the water, whose water you
are stealing from them. This can become such a big
issue that it will be talked about for decades to come, people will
make movies about it,
and it will become part of your history.

Do not look for water in the desert by walking toward the
shimmering horizon. This will kill you. There is no water on
the shimmering horizon. The horizon always shimmers in the
    desert. It is
just the heat dancing.

I had a friend who lived in the desert, at the top of a
windy canyon road. He had a view of the entire city below, and at
night, the city lights. He was my water in the desert, but I
didn't meet him in the desert. I met him in the mountains
above the desert.

Magnetism

I heard that every seven thousand
years the earth's magnetism
belly flops, turns itself inside out. In other words,
the poles change places.

According to the radio announcer, the North
Pole is at this very moment nudging the South
Pole out of its spot.
The poles will pass each other at
the equator, on the way to their
destinations. What will happen the moment they
meet? Will we be compressed into a wedge of energy? And when
    they
overlap, will they twist around each other like a dance? Will one
    move
through the inside of the other's center, like a garment being
turned inside out? Will they spiral past each other like moving
gears? And how will we feel then? Realigned? Inverted?

I wonder how this shifting magnetism makes
us feel. They are moving to replace each other. Already I feel
    skittish,
confused. Already I find myself walking on the ceiling, wearing
    thick
Alpaca sweaters in August. Now the moon comes up in
the mornings. The air is receding into
itself. Soon when I look at you, I will discover that
I have never known you before. At that moment the compass will
    point
down.

Home Movies

Levittown l950s. Begin baby
boom. You're in peach overalls. You look at the
camera, they throw you the ball. They set your toys in front
of you; a stuffed
dog, a plastic lamb, wooden blocks that fit into
their circle and square-shaped holes. You slap at
 the *Levittown Tribune* and sidestep along the marble
coffee table. You wave like a European, squeezing
your hands into fists.

Mom leaves the camera case on. Over the rim
of it I can be glimpsed walking around the back yard, behind
the swing set. I'm holding something, a shovel? The naugahyde
case intervenes. I walk toward the camera, obscuring
myself.

Weaverville. Grandpa disturbs the cow
grazing, it lifts its muzzle into the palm of
his hand. Uncle Bob takes us for rides on a black pony with white
spots. The cow pursues. Mom holds me on the saddle. I raise
my arms out to either side and slip
off gradually. Dad pans the stone house, the hills
beyond, the cow approaching—

Levittown. You rock the hobby horse. I get on it and
ride. You examine your holster. Someone's hat is under the tree. I'm in
Aunt Nunu's lap in my cowboy suit. She claps my
feet together. Janis and your cowboy outfits are brown, mine
is red. She rides the hobby horse with her two dolls

North Bellmore. We stand on the lawn. Robbie touches
my elbow. I'm in a white dress and white
sweater, the present under my arm. It's a long present, expertly
wrapped. I start onto the sidewalk and down the street. I'm
smiling. Robbie follows, running to catch up. He touches
my shoulder and speaks to me. I turn around and
answer. You stand beside the fins of Uncle Arthur's Cadillac and
watch as we stride
by. Robbie is behind me now, forming
a line. He rushes to catch up.

Body Landscapes: Vira Vira—Or the View From Up Here
for KM

Your voice
the landslide
that strands travelers
on either side of a failing bridge

your sad blue eyes
the perfectly round lake
perhaps the mouth of a volcano
extinct now

your scent
the rarefied air
that exhilarates
and kills

your voluptuous mouth
the garden of wild orchids
where I have been left to die
of exposure

the hollow at the base of your throat
the sacred place
where the three rivers
and the three mountain ranges converge

and the view to the east
and the view to the west
and the view to the south

your fingertips
the series of doorways
that were once strung along the cliff
 but have all been destroyed now

by looters, or grave robbers
or conquerors, or blasphemists
or who knows what ravages
of time and memory

your shoulder
the crest of the ridge
the open doorway
where I stand awestruck, looking

and the view to the east
and the view to the west and
the view to the south

your heart
the retreating mule
whose hoof prints
lead me back home

Surf Tanka

The last time I surfed
The moon was out in the morning
The pelicans watched
You were over the mountain
Off on your own adventure

The Hawk

I see the hawk when I
walk along the cliffs above
the beach. He hangs
out in the top of the highest
cypress tree. He flies down the
coast from there, and then
flies back. He has an incredible wing
span. Once I saw him on the roof of
a house, diving
into the garden for a
gopher.

I invest him with
meaning. If I want to see him and
think about it and then I don't see him, I think
it's a lesson about being free
from desire. When I don't
think of him and
do see him, it's a gift. When I want to
see him and
do, I think my dreams will come
true. I think it's good luck. I think I'm in
harmony with the universe and its
power is available to me. When I see him and
he flies, I think I'm lucky, I'm
free, and I'll be able to do
great things, if I only try.

I remember when I first saw him. It was hawk
season, and I'd seen other
hawks in the mountains, and in lighthouse
field, but this hawk was much
bigger. Much
fatter.

Then I started seeing him everywhere.
Once I saw him four days in a row
Now I see him for a few
days, then not, then do
again.

Things That Happen Before an Appraisal:

Birds decorate the
front walkway.
Neighbors take their dog for a
walk and do not clean up after it.

Deer eat the hostas.

You decide at the last
 minute not to take your
realtor's advice, and
stage the house after all.

You go to the grocery
store to buy flowers and realize that it's old
folks day, which means the grocery
store is packed, and by the time you get
 out of there, either *avec* or *sans* flowers, you
will be an old folk too.

You realize that you should
have had the house exterior
power washed and the windows washed.

The new next-door neighbors park three
cars and one truck on their lawn and chop
down the beautiful tree that blocks your view of
the very busy main street two houses away.

Two Aunts

They were both beautiful, both lived
in New York City, both married, both
childless, both international
buyers who traveled the world. One aunt
was blonde and sumptuous, with her hair
pulled back in a French twist like Catherine
Deneuve, the other was dark and spare, with her

hair pulled back in a bun like Coco
Chanel; one was modest, the other
vain; one was affectionate, the other
cold; one was sixty when the other was
thirty; one encouraged me, the other
criticized me; one offered to adopt me, the other
refused me entry to her house; one welcomed my
affection, the other shunned it; one died when I
was in college, the other when I was

forty. They were the yin and
yang of my life—my eternal fulfillment and perpetual
longing, the constellation I revolved around, the vibrating
string to which I calibrated my tune.

Vin Diesel Poem

"we have a little vin diesel in all of us
he implanted himself there in 1947"

the year the yankees won the pennant
the year we got out of germany
and into vietnam

the year my father told my mother
they were leaving queens
and moving to levittown
but my sister wouldn't be born
for five more years

vin, speak to me
your name
diesel truck
win dixie
makes me want to
truck stop
end stop
stop the world
i want to get off

what implants in us
the desire to be human?
it is not a question
I care to ask
1947 is not a place
i care to go back to

they say we have a misconception
of time
i say
only josh knows for sure

You Are What You Eat

I watched in horror a
scientist extract dietary information from the hair of a
4000-year-old Peruvian
mummy. Though they lived by the sea they ate
corn. Corn. It appears that whatever you eat
shows up in your hair a week later, and that
record stays forever, as a last
supper—as it were.

So, for example, if I were to
die today, and my request to be cremated wasn't
honored, and my body was dumped in a
desert, remained preserved, and an
archaeologist found me 4000 years later, hair
intact, and wanted to know what I ate, he would
simply need to put a strand of my hair in a mass
spectrometer, to find out: tamales
with black beans and Monterey jack cheese,
tiramisu, gelato, broad beans, green
salad, oatmeal.

Our Language

In Sanskrit
There are 96 words for love
In Persian 83. In Greek - three
In English only one.

Sometimes I wonder if I speak your language,
if you speak mine.

in whose language should I speak to you?
Should I speak at all?
Sometimes I wonder if we have a language
already
what are the words? what will it entail?

Will our language have passwords?
Will it have private jokes? allusions? innuendo?
Will it be sophisticated and witty? Dry and ironic?
Will it have *Cafe del Rey? Echo Park? Possum? declivities?*
and how many words will it have for love?
how many for regret?
how many for goodbye?

The Clean Room
for CD

There is a room, somewhere
Filled with clean laundry
Stacks and stacks of it
Higher than your wildest heron

There is a desk made from sheets and towels
Lamps folded socks and underwear
Boxers and briefs

A stuffed chair crafted in folded throw rugs and duvet covers
Blankets and pillowcases
button-down shirts stuffed with scarves form the cushions
ties make the stripes.

Likewise there is a sofa of jackets
And a double bed of sweatshirts
Where the boys rest
After chasing the dog catchers
Down Handy Street
as a light snow falls

if you go into the room
alone
and pull up the nightshirt
curtain
and look out onto the deck
you see the outlines
of a future
of boys who want to be
dropped off
of humiliation after humiliation

(to use your words)
of red-eye flights to
Austin
And blue sky nights
Without rodeos
The Alpha puttering in the driveway
Wanting to be
Aired out
On a highway
On a parkway
On the Blue Ridge, maybe

Until
Life reforms
Someone's hand grabs yours
And leads you into a new
Kitchen where

No crumbs
Or doubts
Appear
No dust angels can be made from lying on the floor
And wildly swirling your arms in the
Dog hair
intervention is no longer necessary

where
Baldness is the new
Black
And everything
makes sense again

Fric and Frac2 Fricassée: or the Subtextual Frog
a postmortem for Nina—
(because she likes them)

Things to remember: (in no particular order)
Frogs can be poisonous
they can emit frequencies
Nina is not coming on to you
Nicole is leaving Wednesday morning at 5 A.M.
but she doesn't want to
In five of seven of the poems Alan read tonight
someone was naked
If you have an appetizer you cannot have dessert
you can eat the guest's dessert
but only if they offer you a spoonful

Do not eat fish on Monday
that was delivered Thursday
Do not eat farm-raised salmon
the boy-worn van is blue
the frog has a subtext
Chidsey has hypertext
writing is pleasurable as an activity
this is not a poem
this is not a pipe
 Chidsey has been heard

Driving with Eloise

1.
She drives fast
and sure and
if you look out the window
you can hear her voice
as it was
on the phone
when you first met her
hours and hours trying to keep her on
not let her go
but now she can't go
unless she stops the car
and gets out
and walks away
and so
you are
secretly
selfishly
content now.

You want to turn the radio up loud
roll down the windows
thrust your arms out into the breeze
but you don't
you don't
because there's no time.
because she's a stranger
and even though you've never felt so comfortable
before
Eloise is still a stranger
even when she's driving.
You know. You don't have to remind yourself

It's not like when people say
I feel so comfortable around you
it's like I've known you for years.
It's more like:
I've never felt so comfortable around anyone
even people I have known for years

2.
Eloise is late
but you're not worried
you don't mind.
You know she'll drive up
eventually
and you'll get in
and she'll drive away
maybe without even
looking at you
the way sometimes
when she phones
she doesn't even
identify herself
because she knows
you know
her voice
and you know it's right
and you know it's as it should be
and the second drive is better
because you have the first now
the first smile,
the first laugh,
the first secret
the first green popsicle

and you still don't know
where in L.A. she grew up
or the dogs' names
or why you want to call her El
or why you're afraid to
but you know
that white is your favorite color
for a car
you know
you have what you wanted
Eloise driving
Eloise next to you
the voice
embodied and so you don't worry
and so you smile
and look out the window
you do not think about the sad times
when you will not be in the car
when Eloise will not be driving

3.
The last drive
is always the saddest
lingering in the car
Eloise relieved
because it's over
and nothing bad
happened
she holds out her hand
the hand she steers with
she looks out the windshield
where there are no cars

moving
and she says
I love to drive
but not like that
that's not driving
and she gives you a metaphor
but you don't repeat it
because it's hers
to keep
you want to say
I can't get out of the car
because I'm content
when I'm near you
you want to say
let's drive up the coast
and I'll turn the radio on
and sing loud
and roll the window down
and thrust my arms out
into the breeze
you want to say
anything
so she won't get off
the phone
but she's not on the phone
she's in the car
and it's her car
so it's up to you
to go

You don't watch her
drive away
you don't know if
you will ever see her
again
but you know
you want to
you know you want
the contentment
of Eloise driving
of the voice embodied.

Later
in your room
you shut your eyes
and you are in the car
again
driving
driving with Eloise.

Laura Marello has written eleven books. Guernica Editions published Laura Marello's first novel *Claiming Kin* in 2010, and her second novel *Tenants of the Hotel Biron* in 2012. Her third novel, *Maniac Drifter*, is forthcoming with Guernica in 2016. Tailwinds Press published Marello's *The Gender of Inanimate Objects and Other Stories* in 2015.

Laura Marello has been awarded a National Endowment for the Arts grant, a Wallace E. Stegner Fellowship at Stanford University, a Fine Arts Work Center Provincetown Fellowship, a Vogelstein Foundation grant and Deming Foundation Grant. She has benefited from writer's residencies at MacDowell, Yaddo, Millay, Montalvo and Djerassi.

Laura Marello has taught creative writing at Stanford University, University of California Santa Cruz, University of Oregon, University of Colorado Boulder, University at Albany, Antioch University Los Angeles, and most recently at Lynchburg College.

www.ingramcontent.com/pod-product-compliance
Lightning Source LLC
LaVergne TN
LVHW091235080426
835509LV00009B/1286